C for Coding

Are you too young to coding and feeling like sometimes you can't even follow what is discussed? Or have you already seen some in school but are still feeling frustrated because there are so many new programming features you have never seen? In the modern digital era there are many new stuff popping up on a daily basis. Still, they can become fairly easy to learn if there are straight forward explanations available to get you started. This is exactly what we have prepared for you here - plain-English introduction of the fundamental programming terms you need to know to survive your coding classes. This book focuses on coding related tech terms and phrases that are NOT programming language specific. It is worth taking your time to learn these stuff before getting into the ins and outs of any modern programming language.

Table of Contents

operating system

It is the most important program that runs on a computer. Every computer must have an operating system to run other programs. It performs all the basic tasks.

The software programs you write are going to run on top of an OS, without exception.

low-level languages

They are languages that involve numerous technical details for dealing with the execution semantics of a computer architecture.

These languages are often hardware specific and are very difficult to learn.

high-level languages

They are languages that do not require dealing with the execution semantics of a computer architecture.

These languages are NOT hardware specific and are much easier to learn.

Modern cross platform languages are often high level languages. Scripting languages are mostly high level languages.

top-down

It is a style of programming where a program is constructed starting with a rather high level (in other words, non-detail) description of what it is supposed to do, and then breaking it into simpler smaller pieces.

Simply put, you start with a big picture first.

bottom-up

This approach involves starting from ground zero and learning one thing at a time. You learn the small building blocks first, then later on put these blocks together.

procedural

Procedural programming is a linear process - it uses procedures and/or subroutines to perform computation on the data. The procedures and data are separate entities. You need to plan all the actions and computations at design time. It follows a traditional view that a program is simply a collection of functions or instructions to the computer.

event driven

With event-driven programming, procedures are run only in response to events at runtime. You do not plan ahead when they are run.

Events are typically user interaction related, such as mouse clicks, keyboard press, arrival of data...etc.

Copyright 2020 **Tomorrowskills.com**.

object oriented

People refer to it as OO. An object contains both procedures and data.

OO is not just a way of programming. It is also a way of thinking, or a mindset for planning a program.

The procedures are known as methods in the context of OO programming.

object

You may think of an object as a miniature self-contained component of your program. Objects act on each other by receiving messages, processing data, and sending messages to each others.

class

You may think of it as a set of objects that share a common structure and behavior.

In languages like C++ and C#, a class is a program.

Class variables represent the state of an object of the class.

abstraction

It is an OO concept that calls for removing non-essential characteristics by hiding all but the relevant data about an object. The goal is to reduce complexity and improve efficiency.

Practically, being too abstract can make codes difficult to understand....

integrated development environment

Often being referred to as IDE, this is a complete software for writing and compiling programs.

Modern IDEs are always "visual" - that is, there are visual tools and wizardry interfaces for automating some programming tasks.

visual editor

Traditional code editors are like notepads that require you to type out everything. Visual editors make things easier by allowing you to visually design some parts of the program. The editors are capable of generating codes based on your visual creation.

runtime

It describes the time when the program runs. A runtime environment is what manages program execution for a particular language.

Common language runtime CLR is sort of a virtual machine with the goal of sustaining a particular programming language framework and manage program execution.

interpreter

An interpreter provides a runtime environment for language code that cannot be compiled into executable.

Python, for example, requires an interpreter in order to run.

alerts and errors

Some program errors are difficult to detect until you actually run the program - they are known as runtime errors.

Errors can halt program execution.

Alerts are raised when when there are minor problems that are not problematic enough to halt the program.

syntax

Every programming language has its own set of rules that describe how program statements should be written.

Syntax is like grammar. If you break the grammatical rules, you will experience design time error. Syntax errors are simply grammatical errors but not logical issues.

bug

It refers to an error, flaw, mistake, failure, or fault in your codes that can prevent the program from working as intended.

A bug can arise from unintentional mistakes and errors. Unlike syntax error that can be pinpointed at the time you edit your codes, a bug needs to be "caught" carefully.

debug

It describes the process of identifying and removing errors from your program. It is a boring and time consuming process.

In the practical real world, a program can hardly be 100% bug free.

beta test

Beta testing is the "almost final" testing prior to formal program release. As the last stage of testing, it normally involves sending the program to outside beta testers for real-world exposure and usage.

sandbox

It refers to a "place" to run a program for testing or experimenting. It is an isolated area so anything wrong with the program being tested will not affect the system at all.

btree

It means Binary Tree, a special data structure in which each node has two children. There is one root pointer that points to the topmost node in the tree. There are left and right pointers that recursively point to smaller subtrees on either side.

It is commonly use for searching data.

pseudocode

You can think of it as an informal set of description on what a piece of code does. It describes your program codes in a compact and high-level manner that is fairly easy to understand.

It is typically written in regular English (using English-like keywords and phrases) with a logical or mathematical style.

algorithm

This refers to a special computational method specifically designed for achieving a specific goal, or a procedure for solving a problem with specific actions to be executed in a specific manner and order.

Encryption and sorting always involve the use of special algorithms.

encryption

This refers to the act of scrambling information in such a way that hackers can hardly find out the exact content of the information.

To encrypt an information, special computational methods are required.

sorting

To sort information elements. Different sorting methods require the use of different computational methods.

In programming, sorting is usually performed on arrays.

array

It is like a chain link of data. Think of it as an item that carries a sequence of values, and it always counts from 0. The values being carried are usually of the same type.

See the examples below, the first one is a 1dimentional array. The second one is a 2D array:

int mark[5];

float markreal [5,5];

Copyright 2020 **Tomorrowskills.com**.

type

It tells the kind of variable values you are dealing with. Integer, float, string ...etc are examples of type.

When a program is strongly typed, that means there are very strict rules on the processing of variable types that you must follow.

variable

A variable keeps a value that can be changed.

Data and information are values that can be contained in a variable. A variable is a container for values. The value inside a variable can always be changed.

In a strongly typed program, you must specify the acceptable type of values.

primitive data types

They are data types built in to the programming language.

Common examples include integer , character , void , and float.

Boolean is special as it is either true or false.

declare

In programming languages that are strongly and statically typed, all variables must first be declared before they can be used in your codes.

An example here, which declares my_age as an integer:

```
int my_age;
```

float

It is real number, or number with decimals.

It is a variable data type of real numbers - that is, numbers with decimals.

Float shorts for Floating points. They are computationally demanding. 3D capable programs usually involve intensive floating point calculation.

integer

It is whole number.

It is a variable data type of whole numbers – that is, numbers without decimals.

When an integer is absolute, that means it carries only positive values.

string literal

A string literal is a string. To be technical, it is a sequence of characters all enclosed in double quotation marks.

You use it to represent text.

A null-terminated string is one terminated with a null character, which is '\0' in most languages.

null

Technically speaking it is a value and also a pointer. In fact, in most languages it is a built-in constant with a value of zero, or a pointer referencing a zero.

When we say a variable is null, that means it has received no value.

void

void means returning no value.

A program function typically needs to return "something".

If you put a void there, that means nothing will be returned by the function.

assignment

You may put a value into a variable via assignment. This involves using an assignment operator, which is the operator used to assign a value to a variable.

An example: myvar = 15 is a very simple assignment with = as an assignment operator that assigns the value 15 on the right to the variable myvar on the left.

operators

Operators are symbols that perform some mathematical or logical manipulation of variable values.

There are many different types of operator. Examples include Arithmetic operators, Relational operators, Logical operators, Bitwise operators, Assignment operators, Conditional operators ...etc.

bitwise operations

These are operations on bit patterns or binary numerals involving the manipulation of individual bits.

A bit is the smallest unit of data in computing.

arithmetic operations

They deal with numerical values.

Commonly used standard arithmetic operators include addition (+), subtraction (-), multiplication (*), and division (/).

conditional operations

They evaluate a condition that is applied to one or two Boolean expressions. The result of such evaluation would be either true or false.

nesting

When a block of codes is contained within another, it is said to be nested.

Nesting is common in program statements.

recursion

It means something is referring to or pointing to itself. Think of it as a method of solving problems by breaking down a problem down into smaller and smaller sub-problems until they are small enough to be solved trivially.

Practically, recursion would likely involve a function calling itself.

loop

It is a sequence of instructions that is to be continually repeated until a preset condition is reached.

Examples include while, for, repeat ...etc.

while and for are available on almost all languages. Repeat is available only in some.

break and continue

Break is a command that can break out of a loop.

Continue is a command that can skip one iteration of the loop and continue with the rest.

These commands disrupt the normal flow of your code and is not always appropriate.

Copyright 2020 **Tomorrowskills.com**.

boolean

A Boolean is a data type with only two possible values, which are true or false.

In some languages, true is 0 and false is 1. In other languages, true can be 1 and false can be 0.

arguments

These are values passed between different program functions. They can be used for carrying important information across different functions.

Sometimes they are being referred to as parameters.

statements

Program statements are the instructions of the programs.

A program can consist of one or more statements. Different types of statements can be written to direct the actions the program performs.

printf and scanf

In modern programming languages, print is not printing and scan is not scanning.

print means displaying.

scan means reading user inputs.

Both printf and scanf are the most well known inbuilt library functions in the C language.

Write, writeline, print and println

C uses printf().

C# uses write() and writeline().

Printf with "\n" means pushes to the next line. Writeline does the same.

Printf without "\n" is the same as write.

Java uses print() and println(). Println means print line. You know what it means.

source code and compilation

The program statements you write are source codes – you can always write and edit the codes.

Compilation refers to the act of transforming your source codes into machine readable format. A compiler is required to do this job.

interpreted

Some computer languages are not compiled. Instead, they are interpreted.

The interpreter is like a player, while the codes you write are scripts that are to be played. Modern interpreters are usually made in the form of virtual machines.

We often refer to interpreted codes as scripts.

directives

These are special instructions inserted into the code to direct or change the way the compiler compiles your code.

preprocessor

It is an early step in the code compilation process. It works as a text substitution tool that instructs the compiler to do required pre-processing prior to actual compilation.

As a form of directives typically preceded by a hash sign, it has been used extensively in the C language.

target

When you compile your source code, you may need to tell the target – that is, what OS your program is going to run on.

Different OS work differently so the compiled programs are always target platform specific.

executables

This refers to compiled programs that can be invoked to run.

Unlike source codes, executables are NOT human readable.

On Windows, executables are usually EXE files.

binaries

Binaries are compiled program files. Some binaries are executables while some are simply library files (i.e. not directly executable).

Binaries that are not executables are typically put together for use by the executables.

Copyright 2020 **Tomorrowskills.com**.

binary compatible

It is a term that describes a situation where data files produced by one program are exactly the same as data files produced by another application at the binary format level. With such compatibility, there is no need to import and export data separately.

compile time error

These are errors found at the time you attempt to compile your codes.

These errors make it impossible to compile the codes.

Syntax errors are almost always compile time errors.

shared library

A library is a collection of resources used (and possibly shared) by computer programs.

When a program uses a library, it can gain the function implemented inside that library without having to implement that function itself. It facilitates code reuse.

static library

It is also known as an archive. It is statically linked. In other words, it is compiled into the final binaries as long as it has been mentioned in the program codes.

dynamic-link library

Dynamic-link library DLL is Microsoft's implementation of the shared library concept.

DLL is "dynamic" because linking is "smart" - it is linked only when being actually used. DLL libraries have the file extension DLL, which are commonly found in Windows OS.

procedure

Functions, procedures, methods ...etc can all refer to the same thing. It is all about being modular when structuring a program.

A procedure may contain small sections of code for performing some particular tasks. A procedure may serve one or more purpose, while a function is often single purpose only.

A simple program may have all codes residing in one place without the need for any other functions, procedures, or methods. For more complicated programs, it is a good practice to be modular.

subroutine

A function is a subroutine. A procedure is also a subroutine.

A typical subroutine can be run anywhere within the program.

import, using, include

These are usually found on the first few lines of your code.

When you need to use functions from somewhere else, you need to specify where to get those functions from.

Java uses import.

C# uses using.

C uses #include.

With Java, you are importing a package.

With C#, you are using a namespace.

With C, you are including a header file.

Regardless of the tech details, the above are

all doing the same thing.

stdin, stdout, stdio

Stdin means standard input.

Stdout means standard output.

Stdio means standard input and output.

Keyboard is always the standard input.

Screen is always the standard output.

C# uses console to represent input and output. Java uses System.in and System.out.

main

Every program has a main. You can think of it as the primary MUST HAVE procedure or function of your program.

main is usually written as main().

In languages like C# and C++, a simple main is usually written as static void main ().

methods

In languages like C# and C++, methods are functions.

Methods can be private or public. A public method is one which can be called by any object in any class. A private one can be accessed by objects of the same class only.

built-in functions

Some functions or methods are built-in. In other words, they are provided by the computer language for accomplishing specific tasks.

function call

A function call specifies which function to call. Along the call all of the arguments that the function requires are provided as well.

return value

A function is often written to achieve something. The return value is the outcome of the achievement.

Most functions can return one value at a time only. On the other hand, not all functions have a return value.

pointer

It is a separate entity pointing to the memory address associated with a variable (any variable). It has been commonly used in C, but is no longer popular in modern newer languages.

Generally, manipulating memory addresses is seen as unsafe.

UB

UB shorts for undefined behavior.

When you execute code whose behavior is not defined by the language specification, this error can occur which can disrupt the current state of the program.

bounds

Buffer overflow can occur when your program tries to access an element of your program that does not exist.

Bound checking is a method that you rely on to defend against buffer overflow when some problematic codes are being run.

asp

Active Server Pages ASP is a server side scripting engine that enables the creation of dynamic and interactive web pages.

It is a programming language for the web.

cgi scripts

Short for Common Gateway Interface, cgi scripts are codes that can be used to add features to your web site such as order forms, guestbooks, and hit counters.

CGI scripts have been available long time ago. They reside on the server and is often server platform specific.

xml

Modern web pages may be created via different languages. Extensible Markup Language (XML) is a general-purpose markup language which is "extensible" as it allows users to define their own tags.

Strictly speaking it is NOT a programming language!

java

It is a programming language. It is also a computing platform. It allows complex programs to run through the web. In fact it also runs on mobile and TV devices.

Java is cross platform - it can run on many different OS and platforms.

ecmascript and javascript

ECMAScript is a scripting-language specification which has been standardized internationally. JavaScript is still the most widely used implementation of ECMAScript.

Javascript is a very popular scripting language commonly found on web based systems and web pages. Most web browsers can run Javascript programs flawlessly. The bottomline - it is NOT Java.

swift and lua

It is a relatively new programming language. Released by Apple, it is for developing native iOS or macOS applications (those that run on iMacs and iPhones ..etc).

Lua is a scripting language that is quite similar to Javascript. It is a popular choice when you need to embed a scripting language in a native application.

C and C#

It is a programming language that has won widespread acceptance for several decades.

As an extension to C, C++ is a general-purpose programming language which is primarily object-oriented.

Objective C is a C variant for developing native iOS or macOS applications.

c# is a modern day variant of the legendary c language. It was developed by Microsoft for the .NET framework. It is now open source.

R

It is a programming language primarily for statistics, graphic representation and data analysis. In other words, it is more for data science application.

python

It is a relatively new programming language which is found to be very useful for web services, metaprogramming, data science and machine learning.

It is primarily a scripting and automation language. It is not compiled but interpreted.

ruby

It is a high-level language characterized by clean and easily readable code.

Well-written Ruby code statements almost looks like plain English sentences.

visual basic and ASP.NET

It is a legacy third-generation event-driven programming language that comes with a full scale integrated development environment.

It is specifically for Windows applications development. It does not support other platforms.

ASP.NET is highly similar (in terms of

language syntax) to Visual Basic. It is a server side web application development framework primarily for development of dynamic web pages.

.NET framework

It is a software development platform developed by Microsoft for creating applications that run across multiple different Windows Platforms.

It usually has a common language specification CLS that defines how objects are implemented. It also has a Common Type System CTS which sets the standard way of describing types.

The Framework class library FCL is what keeps reusable classes, interfaces, and types.

The ultimate goal is to allow a more standardized way of programming for all Windows environments.

Sample Hello World – C

The code below involves using all the important concepts we have mentioned in the book.

You include the standard I/O as part of the program.

You have a main program.

You have several integer variables with value assigned.

You have a while loop.

Inside the loop there is an if else logic.

You have printf statements to display values onto stdout.

You have enclosed your code as block.

```
#include <stdio.h>
int main()
{
    int a = 1;
    int b = 11;
    int cc = 0;
    while (cc < b)
    {
        cc = cc + a;
        if (cc != 2)
```

Copyright 2020 **Tomorrowskills.com.**

```c
printf("\n Hey world! Integer value is %d\n" , cc);
else
printf("\n I was told to show something different when
cc is 2");


    }
}
```

The result:

```
Hey world! Integer value is 1

I was told to show something different when cc is 2
Hey world! Integer value is 3

Hey world! Integer value is 4

Hey world! Integer value is 5

Hey world! Integer value is 6

Hey world! Integer value is 7

Hey world! Integer value is 8

Hey world! Integer value is 9

Hey world! Integer value is 10

Hey world! Integer value is 11


...Program finished with exit code 0
Press ENTER to exit console.
```

Sample Hello World — C#

The code below involves using all the important concepts we have mentioned in the book.

You are using the system namespace as part of the program.

You have a class and a main program.

You have several integer variables with value assigned.

You have a while loop.

Inside the loop there is an if else logic.

You have statements that display values to the console.

You have enclosed your code as block.

```
using System;
class HelloWorld {

  static void Main() {
    int a = 1;
    int b = 11;
    int cc = 0;

    while (cc < b)
    {
```

```
cc = cc + a;
if (cc != 2)
{
    Console.Write("Hey world! Integer value is ");
    Console.WriteLine(cc);
}
    else
    Console.WriteLine("I was told to show something different
        when cc is 2");
}
}
}
```

The result:

```
Hey world! Integer value is 1
I was told to show something different when cc is 2
Hey world! Integer value is 3
Hey world! Integer value is 4
Hey world! Integer value is 5
Hey world! Integer value is 6
Hey world! Integer value is 7
Hey world! Integer value is 8
Hey world! Integer value is 9
Hey world! Integer value is 10
Hey world! Integer value is 11


...Program finished with exit code 0
Press ENTER to exit console.[]
```

Sample Hello World – Java

The code below involves using all the important concepts we have mentioned in the book.

You have a main class and method.

You have several integer variables with value assigned.

You have a while loop.

Inside the loop there is an if else logic.

You have print and println statements to display values.

You have enclosed your code as block.

```java
public class Main
{
    public static void main(String[] args) {

    int a = 1;
    int b = 11;
    int cc = 0;

    while (cc < b)
    {
        cc = cc + a;
```

```java
if (cc != 2)
{
    System.out.print("Hey world! Integer value is ");
    System.out.println(cc);
}
    else
    System.out.println("\n I was told to show
    something different when cc is 2");
}
}
}
```

The result:

```
Hey world! Integer value is 1

 I was told to show something different when cc is 2
Hey world! Integer value is 3
Hey world! Integer value is 4
Hey world! Integer value is 5
Hey world! Integer value is 6
Hey world! Integer value is 7
Hey world! Integer value is 8
Hey world! Integer value is 9
Hey world! Integer value is 10
Hey world! Integer value is 11


...Program finished with exit code 0
Press ENTER to exit console.
```

Copyright 2020 **Tomorrowskills.com**.

The source code can be found via this link:

http://tomorrowskills.com/2018/04/17/c-for-coding/

END OF BOOK

Please email your questions and comments

to admin@Tomorrowskills.com.